White Water-lily

Blackberry

Chalkhill Blue

Bluebell

Devil's-bit Scabious

Sexton Be

Small Heath

Longhorn Beetle

English Stonecrop

Swan's-neck Moss

Duke of Burgundy Fritillary

Peacock Butterfly

Daisy

Two-spot Ladybird

Striped Hawkmoth

Dog-rose

Cornflower

Rowan

Common Chickweed

Fritillary

Tufted Vetch

Thistle

Dropwort

Green Carpet

For Amy, amazing and
wonderful editor
and friend

Male Fern

For my mother

All
for the
Newborn
Baby

Scarlet Pimpernel

Phyllis Root

Illustrated by
Nicola Bayley

WALKER BOOKS
AND SUBSIDIARIES
LONDON • BOSTON • SYDNEY

The inn was full.

It was cold in the stable,

dark and bare.

But Mary held her baby close,

and when he fussed,

as babies do,

she sang a little cradle song

all for the newborn baby.

Hush now, baby,

In the manger,

Donkey shares

His sweetest hay.

Oxen breathing

Warm beside you,

Keep the winter

Cold away.

Woolly sheep

Kneel all around you,

Make a fleecy

Place to rest.

Wren weaves moss

And leaves and feathers,

Softly lines

Your manger nest.

Fireflies

Like tiny candles

Light the stable

Where you sleep.

Little fishes

In the river

Flash and splash

And laugh and leap.

Roses in the snow

Are blooming.

Sun and moon

Shine in the sky.

Nightingale

Up in the rafters

Sings his sweetest

Lullaby.

Cherry tree

With branches bending

Offers cherries

Ripe and red.

Spider spins

A silken blanket,

Lays it on your

Manger bed.

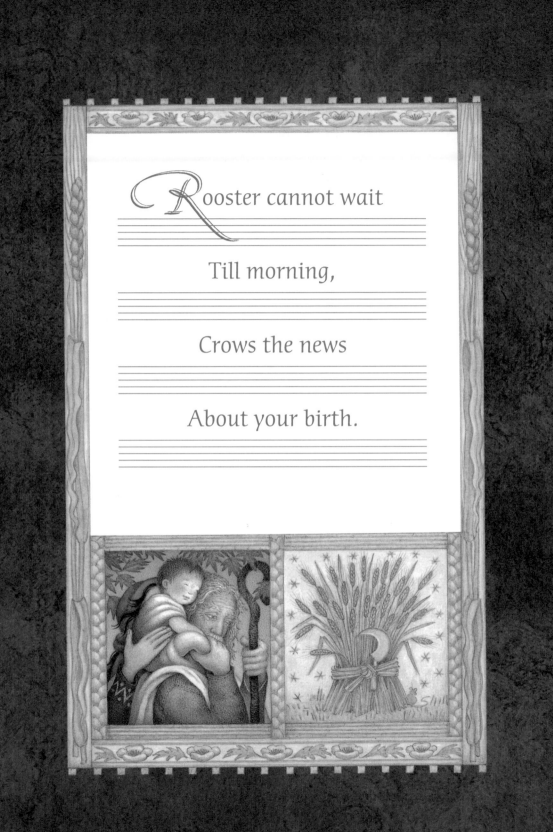

Rooster cannot wait

Till morning,

Crows the news

About your birth.

*H*erons fill the sky

With flying,

Crying *joy*

To all the earth.

$\mathcal{H}$ush now, baby,

In the manger.

All the world

So bright and new

Waits for you, my newborn baby.

Hush and sleep

The whole night through.

Sleep,

my newborn

baby.

Wild Strawberry

First published 2000 by Walker Books Ltd
87 Vauxhall Walk, London SE11 5HJ

2 4 6 8 10 9 7 5 3 1

This book has been typeset in Cerigo Book.
Calligraphic initials by Robin Brockway.

Printed in Hong Kong

British Library Cataloguing in Publication Data
A catalogue record for this book is
available from the British Library.

ISBN 0-7445-4086-0

Birdsfoot

French Marigold

AUTHOR'S NOTE

When I was a child, I read that on
Christmas Eve at midnight the stable animals
speak, and if you are blessed you might
hear them. The image of the animals
talking together stayed with me.
I began to search in old carols and stories
and found more Christmas miracle tales —
donkeys and sheep from many countries, but
especially Italy, oxen from France, a wren from
Belgium, fireflies from England, fish from Puerto
Rico, roses from Germany, a nightingale
from Catalonia in Spain, a cherry tree from
Appalachia in the USA, a spider from Poland,
a rooster from Mexico and herons from Spain.
Slowly these began to weave themselves into
a cradle song that Mary might have sung —
all for the newborn baby.

Swallowtail

Spring Gentian

Hop Trefoil

Hare's-foot Clover

Harebell

Hawthorn

Wild Privet

Heartsease

Heart & Dart

Male Firefly

Hops

Reed Dagger Caterpillar

Green Lacewing

Six-spot Burnet

Large White

Lady's Smock

Ivy

Lime-speck Pug

Shepherd's Purse

Grape Hyacinth

Ivy-leaved Bellflower

Large Tortoiseshell

Ribwort Plantain

Sheep's Sorrel